My First Book About Ducks

Amazing Animal Books
Children's Picture Books

By Molly Davidson
Mendon Cottage Bo

GW00775760

JD-Biz Publishing

Download Free Books!
http://MendonCottageBooks.com

Read More Amazing Animal Books

Purchase at Amazon.com

Download Free Books!
http://MendonCottageBooks.com

Table of Contents

Introduction

Ducks live all over the World, except in Antarctica.

What are ducks?

All ducks can fly, but not all live in the water.

Five white ducks walking

Ducks are not geese or swans.

An adult boy duck is called a Drake, a girl adult is a duck or a hen, and a baby duck is called a duckling.

Ducks get there name from the way they "duck" under the water to eat.

What do ducks look like?

Ducks have long necks compared to other types of birds.

Muscovy Ducks

They also have webbed feet to help them swim.

Ducks also have bills, which are used for eating; ducks also breathe through their bills, with two small nose holes on top.

Boy ducks have colorful feathers, unlike the girls, most baby ducks look like girls, because the boys haven't got there adult feathers yet.

A boy mallard duck

Ducks and what they eat

Ducks eat in two different ways: diving and dabbling.

The Baikal teal duck, also known as a bimaculate duck or a squawk duck. They are dabbling ducks.

Diving ducks are heavier than dabbling ducks, and will dive underwater to get food, they live mostly at sea.

Diving ducks eat mostly fish and mollusks (shell fish).

Dabbling ducks turn upside down to get food; they live in calmer waters, and their feet are smaller.

Dabbling ducks eat plants found under the water.

Dabbling ducks have a strainer in their mouth, so the water will run out and the food will stay to be swallowed.

How ducks act

Black-bellied whistling tree duck

Ducks molt their feathers every year, the old feathers fall off, so they can grow new ones.

Most ducks migrate every year, they travel from north to south and back again. This is to escape the cold weather of winter; most ducks aren't made to survive freezing temperatures.

Ducks lay eggs, about once a year, and when the eggs hatch, the ducklings are immediately brought to the water by the mother.

Ducks and humans

Ducks have been friendly to humans for thousands of years.

Ducks eating feed

Humans keep ducks for meat, eggs, and feathers.

Ducks are much more popular in China than anywhere else.

Ducks that are pets do not like to sit on their eggs and wait for them to hatch, like wild ducks do.

Duck eggs are blue-green to white in color. They are about the size of chicken eggs.

Mallards

Mallard ducks are the ducks from which almost all pet ducks come from.

A group of mallard ducks

Mallards live all over the World.

Boys have green, shiny heads, and brown wings, and girls are brown and speckled all over.

Mallards live in wetlands, and they can live in fresh water or salt water.

Mallards can breed (have babies) with almost any kind of duck, this will make a whole new type of duck.

Muscovy ducks

Muscovy ducks live mainly in Mexico, Central America, and South America.

A pair of Muscovy ducks

Boy Muscovy ducks are two times bigger than girls.

Muscovy ducks have a red or black patch above their beak that has no feathers.

An interesting fact about Muscovy ducks is that they do not migrate. They can handle very low temperatures.

Muscovy ducks don't quack, though they do make noise.

Ring-necked ducks

Ring-necked ducks are diving ducks.

They eat plants, under water and above water, but ducklings eat things like insects and worms.

Ring-neck ducks live in North America.

These ducks migrate to the south, but some are said to be vagrants, they migrate to Britain and Ireland, which is not normal for these birds, but a few do it every year.

Mandarin ducks

Mandarin ducks live in Asia.

A boy and girl mandarin duck

Mandarin ducks will land high in trees and stay there.

The boy mandarin ducks are very colorful, the girls are just spotted brown.

Mandarin ducks will eat many things, in the summer, they eat frogs, small snakes, and worms. In the winter, they will eat corn and grain seeds.

Mandarin ducks will stay a girl /boy pair for life.

Pink-eared ducks

Pink-eared ducks live in Australia.

They are sometimes called zebra ducks due to their stripes.

Pink Eared Duck Wikimedia Commons

They are called pink-eared ducks because of a small pink spot that is on their heads.

They eat plankton and other small animals.

Pink-eared ducks work together to catch food, they will swim in a circle, really fast, then all the plankton/other small animals will be sucked into this water tunnel, so the ducks can eat.

Hottentot teals

Hottentot teals live in Africa and do not migrate.

Hottentot teals will have babies all year round, but only if there has been enough rain.

The ducklings leave the nest when they are only a few days old, and the mother does not help them anymore, they are left by themselves.

Swans

Swans are some of the largest flying birds.

Swans are related to ducks, but they are not a duck. They have long necks and teeth, unlike ducks who don't.

Swans eat frogs and fish.

Swans can have black, orange, or red beaks.

The adult boys are called a cob, adult girls a pen, and the babies are called swanlings.

Swans live mostly in the Northern United States.

Geese

Geese are also a relative of ducks, they are bigger than ducks, but smaller than swans.

A Canadian goose

Canadian geese migrate in a V-shape formation, and eat plants.

Geese are kept as pets for meat, feathers, and eggs.

Geese are meaner in fighting away predators than ducks.

Conclusion

Ducks have been around for thousands, possibly millions of years.

Ducks are amazing creatures, and we're lucky to have them.

Our books are available at

1. Amazon.com

2. Barnes and Noble

3. Itunes

4. Kobo

5. Smashwords

6. Google Play Books

Download Free Books!
http://MendonCottageBooks.com

Publisher

JD-Biz Corp

P O Box 374

Mendon, Utah 84325

http://www.jd-biz.com/

Printed in Great Britain
by Amazon

78635391R00022